THE GIFT OF
NATURE

Inspiring hope and resilience

Catherine DeVrye

ROCKPOOL
PUBLISHING

DEDICATED TO SALLY
a homeless woman in Seattle who wrote
that the words in *Hope Happens!* helped
her get back on her feet.

Since the dawn of time there has always occurred (and probably will always) the darkest of disasters in both Mother Nature and human nature. Thankfully, few of us ever face tragedy that strikes with the strength and speed of tornadoes and tsunamis, or the ferocity of floods and forest fires. Yet most of us do confront crises, real or imaginary, that can instantly change the course of our lives and eclipse not only our dreams but also our desire to carry on. I know because I've been there. Such is the power of nature and the random nature of life.

Although the 'f' is often omitted, shift happens – not only in the fault-lines of the Earth but also in the faults and frailties of its inhabitants. But

the most horrific events can often stimulate us to grow stronger, acting as a fertiliser for consciousness to germinate seeds of hope and optimism. Like tiny seeds with potent power to push through tough ground and become mighty trees, we hold innate reserves of unimaginable strength. We are resilient.

During waves of change or winds of woe, when our clarity of thinking vanishes, lessons from a wondrous array of natural resources can help clear the mental fog and better cope with challenges. Gazing at the galaxy reminds us that, although we are only tiny specks, little things can make a big difference in perception. The inspirational insights I have collected here have given me the inner strength to bounce back and continue my journey in times of deepest despair. I hope at least one of these pages, with my favourite quotes and photographs from nature, will likewise resonate with you.

As my Scottish grandfather used to say, 'It's okay to be down in the dumps, lassie. Just don't stay there too long.' It's not a question of whether you'll ever need to be resilient, but when. Tragedy strikes everyone sooner or later. In my case, it happened to be sooner. I started life in an orphanage, lost both adopted parents to cancer the year after university graduation, faced that dreaded disease myself and fractured a vertebra, to be told I would never play sport again. I could never have imagined I'd be privileged enough to visit every continent on earth.

These days I share my journey with audiences around this weird and wonderful world, who often ask, 'Who or what motivates the motivator?' The answer is simple – nature is my nurture. This may be surprising because I've been struck by lightning in the Australian outback, nearly drowned in a raging river and was lost in a white-out during a Canadian blizzard.

I have experienced earthquakes in Japan and felt the force of an avalanche in the Himalayas. In spite of this handful of lucky escapes, nature constantly bequeaths breathtaking wonder and joy. I've climbed in the sublime silence of the Antarctic and in the Himalayas beyond Everest Base Camp, appreciating that we all face our own 'Everests' in everyday life. Rather than make mountains out of molehills, I've discovered that it's best to tackle any challenge one step at a time – even when it seems there may be one too many rocks in our backpack.

When feeling despondent, the support of close friends is invaluable. Another vital source of strength emanates from nature. It's easy to forget that nature offers many of the best things in life for free. Even in dire economic times, it is possible to turn stumbling blocks to stepping stones with no cost, other than the emotional investment to view things differently.

Like the planet itself, our home and work environments constantly spin and change. Some changes may be dramatic, in the form of mass redundancies or financial woes, sending tremors of fear sweeping through a community as if impacted by a tsunami. More often, it's the ripple-like impact of relatively minor change that can make us feel threatened and disempowered.

As we mature, our resistance to change may increase – or, worse still, develop into complacency about the 'good old days'. But constant change has become the norm and future success will belong to those who not only understand the principles of change, but internalise and embrace such principles in everyday life. The ability to thrive on change, with reserves of resilience, is vital to all organisms. It seems no longer simply survival of the fittest, but survival of the wisest and the most adaptable.

The human well of forward thinking, innovation and imagination remains

virtually unlimited, and often untapped. When we think of natural resources, it's important to remember that every person is also a non-renewable natural resource. Too many of us ignore the fact that we need replenishment and renewal. Too many times, we fail to fully appreciate both the finite and infinite resources not only of planet Earth but also of ourselves.

When we speak of harnessing energy, we must never overlook the harnessing of human energy and potential, both within each of us individually and collectively. This is energy that we personally generate, empowering us to reduce physical and spiritual waste.

Both nature and time have a unique way to rejuvenate and heal us if we allow space in our lives for this to happen, rather than wait until illness or injury forces unscheduled rest.

Apart from the oft-undervalued tonic of sleep to renew finite supplies of

energy, what might we do to recharge ourselves? The more noise pollutes and contaminates, the more we need to escape and recharge, if only momentarily, from the 'high tech' to the 'high touch' environment of nature. Amid my busy calendar, the ability to recharge always comes from solitude in nature. Swimming in the ocean most days defogs my brain. As sand seeps between my toes, I sometimes wish the tide could wash away troubles as quickly as my footprints vanish. I think of my friend Hazel Day who swam in the Pacific every day until she was 91 and claimed that 'Doctor Salt' was the only medication that kept her buoyant. But, of course, it's not quite that simple.

I took health and nature for granted until 1988 when I was stranded in the Thar Desert, bordering Pakistan and India, near the tiny town of Jaisalmer, suffering from bronchitis. I could barely breathe amid swirling sand and was confined to a tent to glean some little relief from the scorching

sun. Once the antibiotics kicked in, I realised that one of the 'old' women who maintained the tent was, in fact, younger than I. Her skin was so dry and shrivelled. The landscape was drier than the woman's prune-like hands – her four-year-old son had never seen rain. Where there was once a large lake, precious water was now hauled from wells many miles away by women in coloured robes with urns and vases balanced on their heads.

I was overwhelmed by guilt at the mammoth effort required to provide me with a drink of water or a wash – simple things that we just expect. In that dusty tent, I vowed to never again take for granted my own health, or the wonder of water. From that day on, I have never let the tap run while brushing my teeth or failed to collect my shower or bath water in a bucket to use later on the garden.

Water shortages have become a stark reality. In 2007 I trekked to

Timbuktu, the ancient city in Mali in northwest Africa. Once a major Islamic centre of learning and trade, where camel caravans found an oasis from their trek south across the Sahara Desert, it is now little more than a dusty town where people try to eek out a living. The Niger River, the third largest in Africa, was once the lifeblood running through Timbuktu but it is now 12 miles away, swallowed by sands that encroached on the city year after year.

Being attuned to the delicate harmony in our environment can enable us to contribute to the well-being of this precious planet. The media is swamped with information on climate change – without doubt, one of the big issues. Some naysayers will claim the sky is too blue, the grass too green, the air too fresh or the water too clean. But, let's face it, respect for the environment is everyone's responsibility. People have varying levels of personal commitment – and cynicism – to social and environmental issues.

But we all need air, water and food for survival. Anything beyond this is only what we want.

I don't pretend to comprehend the depth of scientific research that suggests we can no longer take Mother Nature for granted but I have quietly followed my own environmental conscience for over three decades. Our thanks must go to environmentalists like Sir David Attenborough, David Suzuki and Jean Michel Cousteau who have dedicated their lives to preserving our planet. However, as only one of seven billion inhabitants, I am determined to do my bit a little better. I honestly don't know whether the small things I do make a difference – but they do make a difference to the way I feel about myself.

The Gift of Nature is about learning lessons from nature – and from the changing state of the environment – in order to develop resilience and rediscover the joys of life during joyless times.

Having a purpose or a goal contributes to resilience – especially if it is greater than your own self-interest. Nelson Mandela conceded that, without the time he spent in prison thinking about the possibility of eventual release, he may not have developed the strength to lead his country. While looking forward to the birth of a grandchild or graduation from college may not register quite on the same scale as the rebirth of a nation, it is important to focus on and grasp some sense of meaning in our own particular circumstances.

Many survivors of holocausts, hurricanes or hostage situations viewed these events as temporary and did not remain hostages to their own negative thoughts. An African refugee interviewed on radio after her home was ruined in the Queensland floods of 2011 said, 'It is not so bad. Once we lost our entire village when terrorists burned it to the ground. Many of my friends died of famine. Flood is bad, but fire and famine are worse.'

It is possible to offer aid to individuals in peaceful, stable countries who sometimes feel somewhat short of resilience. Yet what about entire nations which have no choice but to be resilient after their ordinary world is totally disrupted by natural disaster or war? In my own lifetime, I immediately think of Vietnam, Rwanda and Croatia. Sadly, there are many others. I recently visited a makeshift Syrian refugee camp in Serbia, which was once a city park across the street from my comfortable hotel. Hundreds of Syrian refugees were camped there. Their lives had been much like my own before the civil war in their country – they were doctors, teachers, tradesmen, accountants and small business owners. It's impossible to imagine or ignore how tough it must be for those who have had entire libraries destroyed, those who will never visit their local bookstore again or go to their favourite cafe or get to choose the right school for their children.

It's laudable and important for us to somehow keep in perspective that there is always someone worse off than ourselves. But that doesn't make our own challenges any less real – we still must work through them on a practical level wherever and in whatever circumstances we live. Inner courage, at times invisible, shines brightly not just behind enemy lines but during prolonged battles with cancer or other insidious diseases that silently creep up on our immune defences. No one is immune to tragedy.

From my time on the board of the third largest police service in the world, I witnessed the trauma of traffic accidents, theft and fraud, and was sickened by sexual abuse and other heinous crimes perpetrated by the very worst of human beings.

I also witnessed how the human spirit endured through these situations. Volunteering with street kids in Vietnam or Africa, I've seen firsthand how

resilience resounds in many devastated, war-torn lands. Hope can still be found where it is least expected.

Nature heeds no creed, colour or community to transcend genders, borders, politics and centuries. She continually teaches us about what it takes to survive in the world. If only we'd listen. We can indeed learn timeless lessons from nature. In fact, research from leading universities documents scientific evidence that time spent amidst nature can benefit mental well-being.

If you are in need of a bit more hope, open any page at random and you'll be surprised that whatever you read may be most relevant. It's no coincidence that this book is in your hands – because your life is also in your hands and, when times are not brilliant, you must stay resilient.

ARGENTINA

Those who contemplate the beauty of the earth find reserves *of strength* that will *endure* as long as life lasts.

RACHEL CARSON

Believe it or not, YOU have

more inner strength than

you think, so ...

IRELAND

Come forth into the *light* of things, let nature be your teacher.

WILLIAM WORDSWORTH

Like you, every living being

encounters troubled times

from time to time, but ...

LAOS

Out of
difficulties
grow miracles

JEAN DE LA BRUYÈRE

Our external and emotional

environments constantly

change and evolve, but ...

GREECE

Wherever you go, no matter the weather, always bring your own *sunshine.*

ANTHONY J D'ANGELO

Because throughout the

ages, there have been

dark ages and times of

enlightenment, yet ...

JAPAN

Three things cannot be hidden for long. The sun, the moon and the *truth*.

BUDDHA

Nature can inspire hope and

resilience if you honestly face

up to inevitable problems –

and potentials – placed in your

path because …

JAPAN

Life mirrors nature. Some of it's tragic but most of it's *magic*.

Catherine DeVrye

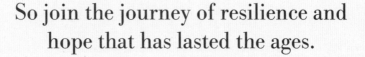

So join the journey of resilience and hope that has lasted the ages.

On the following pages you'll find quotes, photos and poems, plus gentle blank space to pause and reflect on the pathway you face.

AUSTRALIA

Trees, flowers, grass *grow* in silence. See the stars, moon and sun and how they move in silence.

MOTHER TERESA

Electricity can recharge my devices but only nature has sufficient power to recharge my *soul*.

Catherine DeVrye

PALAU

Study nature. Love nature.

Stay close to nature.

It will *never* fail you.

FRANK LLOYD WRIGHT

PALAU

NATURE'S GIFT

The gift of nature is all around –
within our sight, within our sound.

It's there for all the world to see.
It's there for you, it's there for me.

In times of joy or times of strife,
It touches hearts. It touches life.

There are seasons of joy and those of grief
that challenge our courage and strongest belief.

Still, there's hope within each budding bloom
that can help to brighten the darkest gloom.

If facing heat with flames and fire,
you'll be surprised what might inspire.

Mother Nature is full of wonders and woes,
And so too, humans have our highs and lows.

All living things share some connection,
and all human beings have some fear of rejection.

Don't let anyone erode your respect.
If it isn't your truth, don't let others project.

We've all lost some love and misplaced our dreams,
So seek your solace in life's gentler streams.

Whether waves of wonder or those of woe,
It's not just where you've been, but where you can go.

Imagined typhoons of troubles while we lie in our beds,
Catastrophic cyclones rage through our heads.

When thoughts become twisted as tornadoes on plains,
Hang tight to those values which must never wane.

A landslide may find you slip into sorrow,
But hold on to hope for a more stable tomorrow.

When tempers erupt like volcanic ash,
Remember like lava, this too shall pass.

When caught in a blizzard of deepest despair,
Stay calm and consider what options lie there.

When dreams hit a drought or when flooded with tears,
Nurture your soul until fog and mist clear.

From the depths of the sea to the height of the sky,
Most of us search for the what, who or why?

Yet each season unfolds in the fullness of time,
A landscape of lessons so utterly sublime.

Nature's gift is worth more than gold.
She says to all, 'Be brave! Be bold!'

With this gift of the present, we learn from the past
That through all the ages, most troubles don't last.

Let us learn to appreciate that there will be times when the trees will be bare, and look *forward* to the time when we may pick the fruit.

ANTON CHEKHOV

We may metaphorically divide a lifetime into seasons of spring, summer, autumn and winter, each lasting approximately 20 years. In our 'early spring', we learn only from elders. Then, in our teens, adults seemingly know little – until we mature to recognise how much our parents have learned! As a Baby Boomer, in the autumn of my natural life, I now learn from young adults in their summer season and share their optimism that each individual can make a difference to our planet. In the past, my grandparents in their winter years practised long-engrained environmental habits, not because it was trendy, but because of the absolute necessity to recycle during the Great Depression. Each season has its own lessons of renewal and resilience to model and impart.

USA

No winter lasts *forever*.
No *spring* skips its turn.

HAL BORLAND

Tread softly.

Take one step at a time.

INDONESIA

Most of the shadows of this life

are caused by our standing in

our own *sunshine*.

RALPH WALDO EMERSON

When adrift in turbulent
times, never be too proud
to seek guidance from those
who navigated there before ...

ANTARCTICA

Like melting ice, most fears

that freeze our soul will

thaw in the spring.

CATHERINE DEVRYE

Breathe ...

Life is not about waiting for the storms to pass ... it's about learning how to *dance* in the rain.

ANON

Whether dark skies

or dark times,

whether we like it

or not ...

If there were no clouds,
we would not *enjoy* the sun.

ANON

Open your eyes and your

heart to the beauty

of nature ...

Keep your face to the *sunshine*

and you cannot see the shadows.

HELEN KELLER

Nature has always adapted to harsh environments. We too must trust our survival instincts.

You never know your natural strength until being *strong* is the only choice you have.

CATHERINE DEVRYE

We may sometimes feel alone
in the absence – or even in
the midst – of family and
friends, but ...

CHILE

No bird **_soars_** too high if

he soars with his own wings.

WILLIAM BLAKE

At times we may feel weak

and helpless ...

It is not the strongest of the species that survives, nor the most intelligent, but the one most adaptable to *change*.

CHARLES DARWIN

Like it or not, we often must

adapt to difficult changes.

Tragedy is inevitable. *Growth* from tragedy

is optional.

CATHERINE DeVRYE

BOUNCE BACK

Bounce back from trouble. Bounce back from strife.
Setbacks and sorrow are all part of life.

Bounce back from sadness. Bounce back from pain.
Bounce back from failure, again and again.

Bounce back from sickness. Bounce back from grief.
Things always seem worse before sighs of relief.

Bounce back from earthquakes. Bounce back from fire.
Never lose sight of your own heart's desire.

Bounce back from job loss. Bounce back from weight gain.
Keep a stiff upper lip as you dance in the rain.

Bounce back from bullies. Bounce back from thieves.
Seek out true friendship when deepest you grieve.

Bounce back from critics. Bounce back from fear.
Trust most when you doubt a solution is near.

Bounce back from failure. Bounce back from defeat.
It won't be that long till you're back on your feet.

Bounce back from depression. Bounce back from despair.
Not all can be fixed, but most likely repaired.

Bounce back from heartache. Bounce back from pain.
Breakups and makeups, renew yet again.

Bounce back from setbacks. Bounce back from falls.
Never forget that your destiny calls.

Bounce back from disaster. Bounce back from storms.
Such trials and trauma, strong character forms.

Bounce back when tough times seem hard to break through.
Resilience is vital ... it's all up to you!

CATHERINE DEVRYE

Children soon learn that if they drop an apple, an egg or a ball, only one will not bruise or break – but bounce back.

We may have lost the innocence and awe of childhood. However ...

Things do not change; we

change.

And constant

transformation happens

throughout history and

the world.

No one will die in the same world
in which they were *born*.

MARGARET MEAD

Yet young and old will come

to learn that …

MONGOLIA

Resilient beings know that the grass will soon turn just as *green* on their side of the fence.

CATHERINE DEVRYE

There is no comparison

between that which is lost by

not succeeding ...

and that which is lost by not *trying*.

ANTARCTICA

FRANCIS BACON

Trust.

ANTARCTICA

64

You cannot *discover* new oceans until you have *courage* to lose sight of the shore.

ANDRÉ GIDE

Most stumbling blocks

become stepping stones:

Tread onward with purpose

when you feel most alone.

If you

follow

a path with no obstacles it likely

leads nowhere worthwhile.

CATHERINE DeVRYE

Exercise tenacity.

Headwinds on our journey build strong muscles – and *strong* character.

CATHERINE DeVRYE

Move forward however

slowly but surely ...

ECUADOR

The man who is swimming against the stream knows the *strength* of it.

PRESIDENT WOODROW WILSON

We are all part of something

ever-changing and so much

bigger than ourselves.

AUSTRALIA

Solitary trees, if they grow at all, grow *strong*.

We may still feel isolated in

an emotional wilderness.

Stand steadfast.

JORDAN

Should you shield the canyons from the windstorms, you would never see the true *beauty* of their carvings.

ELISABETH KUBLER-ROSS

And timeless wisdom offers

universal truths ...

Every cloud has a *silver* lining.

MUM (AND DOUBTLESS MANY OTHER MUMS)

WHEN THINGS GO WRONG

When things go wrong as they sometimes will,
When the road you're trudging seems all uphill,
When the funds are low and the debts are high,
And you want to smile but you have to sigh;
When things are pressing you down a bit,
Rest if you must – but don't you quit.

Life is queer with its twists and turns,
As every one of us sometimes learns,
And many a failure turns about
When he might have won if he'd stuck it out;
Don't give up though the pace seems slow –
You might succeed with another blow.

Often the goal is nearer than
It seems to a faint and faltering man ...

Success is failure turned inside out –
The silver tint of the clouds of doubt,
And you can never tell how close you are,
It may be near when it seems afar;
So stick to the fight when you're hardest hit –
It's when things seem worst that you mustn't quit.

EDGAR GUEST

Pause to reflect on your

current clouds of concern.

Nature does not hurry

yet everything is

accomplished.

LAO TZU

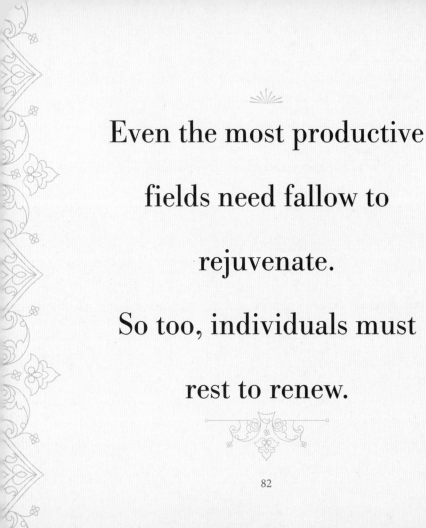

Even the most productive

fields need fallow to

rejuvenate.

So too, individuals must

rest to renew.

A life without dreams is like a garden without *flowers.*

GERTRAUDE BEESE

Pause to ponder ...

Adopt the pace of nature.
Her secret is *patience*.

RALPH WALDO EMERSON

Time heals most

misfortunes. Just

as plants use light energy

to produce oxygen ...

Inhale the *future.*

Exhale the past.

CATHERINE DEVRYE

Isn't it about time to

emerge from that cacoon

of self-pity?

What the caterpillar calls the end, the rest of the world calls a *butterfly.*

LAO TSU

Believe ...

JAPAN

Only when it is dark enough can you see the *stars*.

PERSIAN PROVERB

Visualise new possibilities

for growth ...

There are always flowers for those who want to *see* them.

HENRI MATISSE

Rediscover meaning

and purpose ...

To everything there is a season, and a time to every *purpose* under heaven.

ECCLESIASTES 3:1

Nature discriminates not
amongst nations or creeds.
All have their share
of lessons to heed.

NEW ZEALAND

Nature is a mutable cloud which is always and never the same.

RALPH WALDO EMERSON

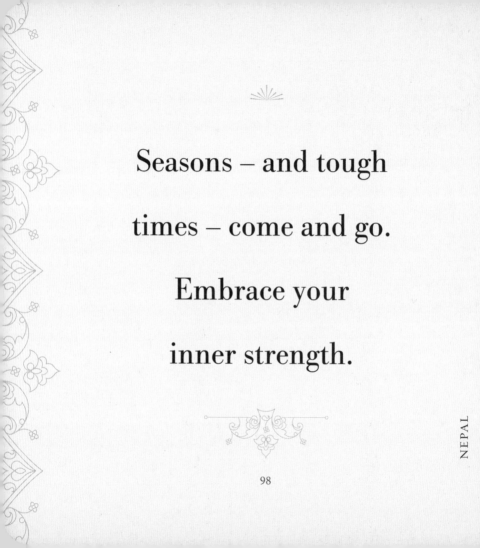

Seasons – and tough
times – come and go.
Embrace your
inner strength.

NEPAL

In the midst of winter, I found there was within me an *invincible* summer.

ALBERT CAMUS

We all get second chances.

CANADA

Autumn is a second

spring

when every leaf is a flower.

ALBERT CAMUS

So look for even the

tiniest emerging glimpse

of beauty.

NEPAL

Never opt out of *optimism.*

CATHERINE DeVrye

There will always be

both days of joy and

those of grief, but ...

FRANCE

Every day above ground

is a *good* one.

FRANK JANSEN

It's easier said than done,

but choose to look on

the brighter side of

sorrow's shoreline.

CHINA

All seasons are *beautiful* for the person who carries *happiness* within.

HORACE FRIESS

I once saw a sign that read:

four out of three people

have mental health issues.

It was meant as a joke but it

is indeed serious because ...

AUSTRALIA

Everyone is a *moon,* and has a dark side which he never shows to anybody.

MARK TWAIN

No one is always on top

of the world – but some

people are better actors

than others.

JAPAN

The best *remedy*

for those who are afraid, lonely

or unhappy is to go outside,

somewhere where they can be

quite alone with the heavens,

nature and God.

ANNE FRANK

Life seldom flows as
smoothly as we'd wish – and
we sometimes feel drowning
in doubt and despair

LAOS

What makes a river so restful

is that it doesn't have any

doubt.

It is sure to get where it is

going, and it doesn't want to

go anywhere else.

HORACE FRIESS

When face to face

with conflict, we may

become stunned and

immobilised.

If you can meet with *Triumph*

and Disaster. And treat those two

impostors just the same ...

RUDYARD KIPLING

Stay calm and focus not

on the problem but on

the potential solution ...

BOTSWANA

Hope is the thing with feathers
that perches in the soul,
And sings the tune without the words,
and never stops at all …

EMILY DICKINSON

Sometimes, it's just a

little glimmer almost

too small to see – so look

more closely ...

Hope is the only bee that makes honey without flowers.

ROBERT GREEN INGERSOLL

Hope and inspiration

may also be found

amidst a field of long

lost dreams ...

THE NETHERLANDS

When flowers *bloom,*

so does hope.

LADY BIRD JOHNSON

Growth.

A *life* without thorns is like a

rose without petals.

CATHERINE deVRYE

Pause to go

inside yourself.

Inside myself is a place where I live all alone and that's where you *renew* your springs that never dry up.

PEARL BUCK

Everything perishes in time,
So laugh and love while you may,
Help who you can,
Work while you must,
And when the end comes, so be it.

All fame ends in oblivion
And is soon forgotten.
But it is fun to strive; joy to win.
It is a challenge to lose and try again.
And victory always comes
If you try hard enough.

To lose is not to fail.
The only failure is to lose
And not try again!

ANONYMOUS

ANDORRA

A river cuts through rock, not because of power, but because of *persistence*.

JIM WATKINS

Be persistent.

Stand strong.

It's not the mountain we

conquer

but

ourselves

Sir Edmund Hillary

Our natural and emotional environments constantly change and the only time 'rainbows' come before 'storms' is in the dictionary.

AUSTRALIA

If you want the *rainbow,* you gotta put up with the rain.

DOLLY PARTON

All creatures great and
small will find that
nature is cruel – but
more often kind.

ECUADOR

The best thing one can

do when it is raining is

to *let it rain.*

HENRY WADSWORTH LONGFELLOW

Still look to the horizon

of hope …

INDONESIA

A single *sunbeam* is enough to drive away many shadows.

SAINT FRANCIS OF ASSISI

Listen closely to the silent

power of intuition ...

USA

A setting sun still whispers a *promise* for tomorrow.

JEB DICKERSON

Don't always wear your heart

on your sleeve, but never be

too proud to ask for help.

AUSTRALIA

Man's *heart* away from

nature becomes hard.

STANDING BEAR

Life is often hard –

until it becomes easier.

When tired of the song

that sorrow sings, change your

tune to find your wings.

CATHERINE DeVRYE

Nurture choice.

Turn your face to the

sun

and the shadows
fall behind you.

Māori Proverb

Learn from the past.

Live in the present.

Look to the future.

ANTARCTICA

Look deep into nature,
and then you will
understand
everything better.

ALBERT EINSTEIN

You'll better understand ...

Life isn't measured by the number of breaths we take, but by the ***moments*** that take our breath away.

ANON

Life ...

Nature often holds up a *mirror* so we can see more clearly the ongoing processes of growth, renewal and transformation in our lives.

MARY ANN BRUSSAT

RESILIENCE

Resilience is something we all have inside:
So often hidden where deep fears reside.

It can spring to the surface in times of despair
Without ever knowing it has long lingered there.

When all hope seems lost and no help is near
Resilience surprises when it does yet appear.

Soothing thoughts flow as gently as streams;
After torrents of trouble that clouded our dreams.

Trees of knowledge from depths of doubt
Strength ebbs and flows – like tides in and out.

Seeds of greatness sown in souls
Around the globe – between the poles.

Nature's lessons rich as gold
Sometimes subtle – sometimes bold.

Full of wisdom – free of charge
Sometimes little – sometimes large.

When breezes whisper or thunder roars
At times brush our surface – at times pierce our pores.

The dawn of morning and dark of night
Seek horizons of hope during times bleak and bright.

Leave nothing but footprints. Take nothing for granted.
Trust the wonder of nature to help faith be re-planted.

We need to accept that life's not always brilliant.
Such are those times to find words of resilience.

CATHERINE DEVRYE

When feeling as insignificant

as a single grain of sand ...

In the midst of a desert of despair, hope remains an *oasis* in the heart.

CATHERINE DeVRYE

We may feel deserted in the

Sahara of our soul but nature

can offer respite from a

seemingly emotional wilderness.

INDIA

What makes the desert
beautiful is that somewhere
it hides a well.

ANTOINE DE SAINT-EXUPERY

You are as unique as any

snowflake, so keep moving on.

Never measure the height of

a mountain until you have

reached the top.

Dag Hammarskjöld

Too often, we make mountains
out of molehills and give up
when our goal is just out of sight
beyond the immediate horizon.

It always seems impossible until it's done. After climbing a great hill, one only finds that there are many more hills to *climb*.

NELSON MANDELA

Whether we view our world from mountain tops to ocean shores, or more likely our everyday urban environment, it's only natural to feel despondent at times.

A life without worry is

like a sea without *waves*.

CATHERINE DEVRYE

The more that noise pollutes and contaminates our time, the more we need to escape, if only momentarily, from the high tech to the high touch surrounds of a natural environment.

AUSTRALIA

You will find something more

valuable in woods than books.

Trees and stones will

teach what you can never

learn from masters.

SAINT BERNARD

Because I have been privileged to

see so much of our world, I wanted

to share some images and insights

that may have a ripple effect on

the shoreline of your future.

ECUADOR

You are a *child* of the universe

no less than the trees and the stars.

You have a *right* to be here.

DESIDERATA

With rights come responsibilities. Like explorers in the past, we now know our planet is neither flat nor her resources inexhaustible so we each have a duty to preserve our natural habitat.

MALI

No pessimist ever *discovered* the secrets to the stars, or sailed to an uncharted land, or opened a new heaven to the human spirit.

HELEN KELLER

Through centuries and seasons,
Mother Nature and human
nature have proved both kind
and cruel. Regardless ...

AUSTRALIA

Part of being an *optimist* is keeping one's head pointed towards the sun, one's feet moving forward.

NELSON MANDELA

When faced with seemingly insurmountable obstacles, there exists that fine line and delicate balance between succumbing or surviving; retreating or rebounding; giving up or getting up to try again.

ARGENTINA

Two things stand like stone –
kindness in another's trouble
and *courage* in one's own.

ADAM LINDSAY GORDON

I'm neither an environmentalist

nor a psychologist, but one thing

I know as an immutable truth ...

When immersed in a sea of

seemingly shattered hopes ...